Macaws and More

By Loren Spiotta

As parrots and parrot-like birds have become more and more popular, the need for information regarding their diet, behavior, and breeding habits has also risen. This book can offer advice on obtaining and keeping macaws, one of the largest and most popular members of the parrot group.

Perhaps the best known of all the parrots, the macaws have proven to be some of the most easily trained birds in captivity, some have even been trained to roller-skate, ride bicycles, work puzzles, and perform tricks. In looks alone, the macaws are stars—the striking solid blue of the hyacinths, the strong

contrast of the blue and gold, the bold beauty of the scarlets. However, these great birds are not just about fun and games; the information provided in this book is designed to educate owners about the time and care required for macaws.

Whether the macaw you choose or already owns proves to be an excellent companion, performer, or even show bird, as an owner you will grow to appreciate your bird's many assets—including its capacity to show true affection to its keeper. This book will provide you with all the information you need to know about keeping your macaw, and it should serve as a useful guide throughout his long life with you.

© by T.F.H. Publications, Inc.

Distributed in the UNITED STATES to the Pet Trade by T.F.H. Publications, Inc., One T.F.H. Plaza, Neptune City, NJ 07753; on the Internet at www.tfh.com; in CANADA Rolf C. Hagen Inc., 3225 Sartelon St. Laurent-Montreal Quebec H4R 1E8; Pet Trade by H & L Pet Supplies Inc., 27 Kingston Crescent, Kitchener, Ontario N2B 2T6; in ENGLAND by T.F.H. Publications, PO Box 15, Waterlooville PO7 6BQ; in AUSTRALIA AND THE SOUTH PACIFIC by T.F.H. (Australia), Pty. Ltd., Box 149, Brookvale 2100 N.S.W., Australia; in NEW ZEALAND by Brooklands Aquarium Ltd. 5 McGiven Drive, New Plymouth, RD1 New Zealand; in SOUTH AFRICA, Rolf C. Hagen S.A. (PTY.) LTD. P.O. Box 201199, Durban North 4016, South Africa; in Japan by T.F.H. Publications, Japan—Jiro Tsuda, 10-12-3 Ohjidai, Sakura, Chiba 285, Japan. Published by T.F.H. Publications, Inc.

MANUFACTURED IN THE
UNITED STATES OF AMERICA
BY T.F.H. PUBLICATIONS, INC.

Contents

Photography by:
Glen S. Axelrod, Dr. Herbert R. Axelrod,
Joan Balzarini, Isabelle Francais, Robert
Pearcy, Carol Thiem

Introduction

The majestic macaws (pronounced ma'kaw') are the largest members of the parrot family. Though there are size differences among the approximately 30 species and subspecies, all macaws have similar characteristics: a large facial area known as a cheek patch. Macaws are extremely hardy birds noted for their longevity; some have lived for more than 60 years.

The macaws' harsh, high-pitched call is often very irritating to the human ear. Fortunately, however, these birds don't give voice all day long. They usually screech only in the early morning or later in the evening. A bored and frustrated macaw will also scream to get attention. A contented bird is much more peaceful.

Despite their harsh natural call, the talking voice of these parrots is quite soft and encompasses a greater range of sound. Though macaws are not usually known for their talking ability, given enough attention and proper training these highly intelligent and playful creatures can develop a good vocabulary. Some talented birds have even become bilingual. However, keep in mind that talking birds cannot comprehend what they are saying. They simply repeat what they hear. You may have been deceived by a parrot when it correctly answered a question asked of it. This is only a conditional response. Most of the credit should be given to the bird's patient and devoted trainer.

Most macaws have brilliant plumage encompassing a great range of color, from the deep rich blue of the hyacinth macaw to the radiant red of the scarlet macaw. These and other popular species will be discussed in greater detail in the last chapter.

Sexing macaws is a difficult task. Males usually have larger heads and broader beaks than females. Yet, because there are no color variations between the sexes, positive identification is always tricky. Some bird owners buy a pair of macaws for breeding purposes and later discover, much to their surprise, that the birds are of the same sex!

Macaws love to chew—it is, in fact, one of their favorite pastimes. Chewing gives the macaw needed exercise for its powerful beak as well as hours of enjoyment. A macaw will chew anything in sight to keep its upper mandible (beak) from becoming too large. Therefore, it is essential that you provide your pet with plenty of wood scraps and a strong wooden perch to fulfill its chewing needs. If your macaw has the run of the house, keep your eye on it, for it will delight in destroying your furniture. Basically,

Macaws can be identified by the presence of a large facial area called a cheek patch, which on blue and gold macaws is white and lined with black.

The brilliant plumage of macaws such as the green winged makes these large parrots extremely popular with bird lovers.

macaws are not very messy, but because of their size and chewing habits they can be a bit more troublesome than some smaller parrots.

Macaws are not for everyone. Each bird has a distinct personality; no two are alike. Some adore men, while others show a marked preference for women. Still others take a liking to children. Many macaws become very attached to their owner and shy away from strangers. It is difficult to say what type of personality your bird will develop, so be prepared for the unexpected.

Though macaws can be as loving as puppies, they can also be extremely nasty. Most vicious birds are a product of manhandling. Though unfortunate, these birds should not be brought into your home unless you have the time and knowledge to undo the damage. Even then you may never be able to transform a nasty bird into a gentle pet. It is therefore strongly suggested that you do not get involved with a problem bird.

Macaws are typically expensive birds to purchase, with some tame birds costing thousands of dollars. Because of their large size and need for activity they must be given ample living quarters. Equally important, macaws must have plenty of human attention if they are to live contented lives in captivity. However, if you have the time and desire to provide for the needs of one of these magnificent parrots, it will undoubtedly become an exceptional pet.

There are many macaws to choose from, including the green winged and the hyacinth.

Macaws, especially hyacinths, have powerful beaks and love to chew.

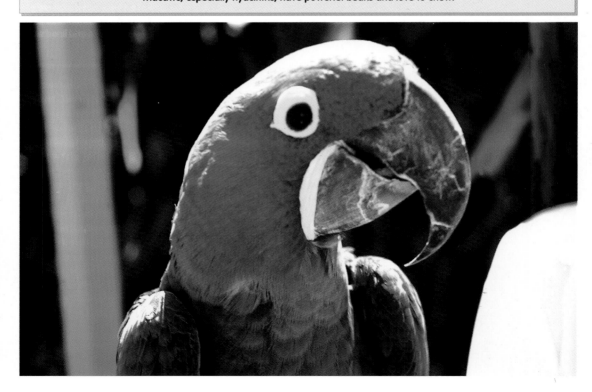

Buying A Macaw

SELECTING THE RIGHT BIRD

Before you actually purchase a macaw, you should learn as much as possible about the different species in order to decide which bird is right for you and your family. There are several factors to consider. Do you have enough room for an adequate-sized cage in your home? A cage for the larger macaws should be no less than 37" high, 24" wide and 25" long. If you don't have enough space, or feel that you might not be able to fulfill the needs of a larger bird, you might decide to buy a dwarf macaw. These smaller versions also make wonderful pets. Are you planning to keep the bird in an aviary year-round; if so, which species can adapt to such an environment? Most macaws should be taken in during the winter months, so it would be wise to know this before you purchase the bird. Do you have children or pets? Some macaws get along well with both, others don't. A macaw can easily injure a child with its powerful beak. Unsupervised children should not be allowed to play with these birds. Do you want a bird that will be a friend to all or one that is strictly devoted to you? Most macaws grow attached to the one who cares for it.

What type of bird can you afford? The hyacinth is a beautiful and gentle creature, but it is also rare and therefore commands a very high price. Do you want a bird that will become a devoted pet or are you only interested in a

Buying a macaw is a lifetime commitment; there are a number of important factors to consider before making a purchase.

flashy centerpiece for your living room? If you answered yes to the second part of this question, perhaps you'd better reconsider buying a bird altogether. A bird, like any other pet, is a living creature. It needs a lot of love and attention in order to live a contented life in captivity. If you cannot or will not give your pet what it needs and deserves from you, it will undoubtedly become bored and frustrated. In time you will have a very destructive animal on your hands. Ignoring a pet bird, especially one as active as a macaw, is the same as sentencing it to a life of futility in a cage no better than a prison. So please carefully consider your reasons for buying a bird.

The last chapter of this book deals with several types of macaws, the behavior of each species in their native lands, their coloring, and also what is known of their behavior in captivity. Although this should give you some basic knowledge of macaws, you should visit local zoos that have these magnificent birds. Study them carefully. Talk to the person who cares for them. Try to find out as much as possible about these birds before you decide which one is for you. Pet shops are also a good place to start. Many pet shop dealers know quite a bit about exotic birds; even if they don't, they should direct you to someone who does. Remember, buying a macaw is a lifetime investment, so make your choice wisely.

Macaws can make excellent additions to your family—
as long as you have the space and time for them.

When choosing a bird, keep in mind that younger birds adapt more easily to new surroundings than older birds.

SIGNS OF A HEALTHY BIRD

Because macaws are large and expensive birds, it would be unrealistic to assume that they are readily available for purchase in pet shops. Indeed, very few pet shops are able to afford to keep a macaw on their premises. However, almost all pet shop dealers are able to purchase a macaw for a seriously interested customer.

In order to have a macaw that will grow into a fine, healthy, and affectionate pet, it is advisable to purchase the bird at a young age, ideally between eight months and one year. A younger bird is even better yet, but it is unlikely that you will find one for sale that is under eight months old. A young bird will be able to adapt more readily to its new owner and surroundings, whereas an older bird already has set habits and may be difficult to train. Though it is not impossible to train an older bird, it does require a great deal more of

time and patience. Those that are bred in captivity are more accustomed to humans and will probably make better pets. So when you order a macaw from a pet shop, inquire about its background.

A pet shop dealer will do the best he or she can to select a young healthy bird for you. However, it would be worthwhile to know a few facts about macaws to make sure your selected bird is indeed young and healthy.

Age and sex in macaws are nearly impossible to determine. The plumage in both sexes is virtually the same and there are no outward discriminating sex factors. Usually the male of a species is larger than the female. A healthy male macaw may also have glossier plumage. For those of you who are interested in the blue and gold macaw, it is said that they blush when agitated. Blushing occurs in the bird's naked cheek patch and is seen more often in the male of the

species. Age is equally difficult to determine. However, watch for gray scaly legs and rough eye rings. These are signs of an older bird.

Fortunately, assessing a bird's health is much easier. A healthy macaw should have bright clear eyes, and its breathing should be calm and steady. Loud irregular breathing is often a sign of lung or respiratory disease. If a bird is having difficulty breathing it will rock back and forth on its perch and lack interest in preening itself.

A macaw's beak should be smooth and not show any signs of unusual growth. Its feathers should be sleek and shiny, tightly aligned to its body. Broken feathers or even a frayed tail aren't that serious because they will grow back. But beware of a bird that appears listless and

Some macaws get along better with children than others. Be certain to supervise play sessions.

Choices abound when selecting the perfect young macaw for you and your family. Pictured from left to right: military macaw, two blue and golds, scarlet macaw.

Many believe that the cheek patch of a blue and gold macaw will blush when the bird is agitated.

fluffed out on a perch. A sick macaw will hold its wings slightly away from its body and its eyes will appear small because its head and face feathers will be ruffled. A bird in such condition is probably suffering from a cold or other ailment.

Macaws are easily stricken with diarrhea (actually a symptom of another problem), so be sure that the bird is not soiled around the vent and that its droppings are firm and not watery.

Though it may sound ridiculous, make sure your bird has all of its toes. Healthy feet are extremely important. If a bird is sleeping on both feet, this is another sign of some disorder, since a bird normally sleeps on one foot. Any bird that has more interest in sleep than play and hides its head in the feathers on its back is also suffering from some malady.

If you are unaccustomed to caring for ailing birds and your selected macaw appears to be ill, you should ask your dealer for another. There is no point in asking for trouble and unnecessary heartache.

COST

There are several factors that influence the cost of a macaw. Among them are size, color, and previous training. An untamed bird will be a lot less expensive, as will a bird with comparatively dull plumage. A pet shop dealer will best be able to tell you about the types of macaws that are available to you and their price ranges. You should deal with a shop you know to be respectable, one that considers the well-being of an animal more important than anything else. By so doing you will increase your chances of obtaining a healthy bird that will enter-tain and delight you for many years to come.

Living Accommodations

MACAWS AS HOUSE PETS

There are a number of ways to house macaws in captivity so that they will adapt readily and happily to domestic life. Your new arrival will be unsure and frightened in its seemingly strange and unfamiliar surroundings, so it makes sense to have its living accommodations already set up before you bring the bird into your home. Having everything prepared beforehand will also help to avoid further inconvenience and confusion.

Like all pet birds, macaws require equipment such as perches, cages, and aviaries.

If you plan to keep your macaw as a house pet, you should begin by purchasing a strong wire mesh or wrought iron cage or a T-perch with a removable wire mesh cover. Either enclosure will give the bird a sense of security and the feeling that this domain is his. Later, when the bird is tame, you can remove the cover from the T-perch if you wish.

A cage for the large macaws should be no less than 37 inches high, 24 inches wide, and 25 inches long. A cage for a hyacinth macaw must be even larger and made of extra-strong metal. It is imperative that the bird should have ample room to stretch its wings. Also, when sitting on its perch, its tail should not be able to touch the floor of the cage nor should its head reach the top. The perch has to be made of sturdy wood, because it will have to hold up under constant chewing.

Proportions of a cage are actually more important than the volume of the enclosure. A cage with greater length

Your new macaw should feel right at home once he's settled in a cage with perches, toys, and water and food dishes.

in relation to its height and width is better than one with equal dimensions. Greater length allows more room for needed exercise. Aside from having enough space to spread its wings, a cage should be wide enough for the bird to hide from a disturbance coming from any direction.

IMPORTANCE OF ADEQUATE HOUSING

The importance of an adequately sized cage cannot be stressed enough. Though it may be expensive to purchase, a good cage is essential for the bird's well-being. If you are an apartment dweller and haven't enough space for a large cage, reconsider your decision to buy a macaw. If you simply can't afford to buy such a cage, perhaps you should select a dwarf macaw or a smaller parrot. A large macaw in an ill-fitted cage can develop numerous behavior problems. To begin with, a bird that feels cramped will try endlessly to escape. Some birds perform countless figure eights. Others bow continually, while others swing their heads from side to side. It's no wonder that these birds quickly become psychologically disturbed.

Macaws need not only a good-sized cage, but also an environment rich in stimuli in order to maintain stable mental health. They need to see, hear, and play with various objects to keep themselves occupied. If denied these things, the bird will become very disturbed and resort to self-mutilation. Feather plucking is a sure sign of a disturbed bird. Some birds pluck themselves almost completely nude. Other birds

chew on their toes, which can result in the loss of a toe or even an entire foot. The saddest problem of all is that once this neurotic behavior is set in motion it is nearly impossible to stop. Yet all of this needless trouble can be avoided if you furnish your

Although caged birds should be allowed room to exercise, you should wait until your bird is tame before letting him roam through your house.

bird with a good cage and ample stimuli.

Don't be afraid to pamper your bird. Buy it as many toys as you like. A change of toys adds novelty to its life. Your pet will love you for it, and you will delight in watching its antics.

Of course, after your bird is tame, you should allow it out of the cage. Most macaws

become lazy when they live indoors, so you may have to encourage your pet to get added exercise. You may decide to allow your pet the freedom of one room or the entire house. Whatever you decide to do, remember to keep your eye on him: a mischievous macaw may well get itself into trouble.

Although many macaws get along well with other family pets, it's best not to force introductions or keep pets together unsupervised. There are accounts of macaws fighting medium-sized dogs to death, the bird being the victor. Never underestimate the power or wrath of a macaw.

Some people choose to chain their birds to a perch instead of allowing it to wander freely. Most feel that this practice is absurdly ignorant as well as inhumane. Obviously, if a bird chained to a perch is frightened, it can easily break a toe or leg in its efforts to escape from harm. Furthermore, a bird should be kept as a pet not a prisoner.

PLAYPENS

Aside from its cage, a macaw should also have a

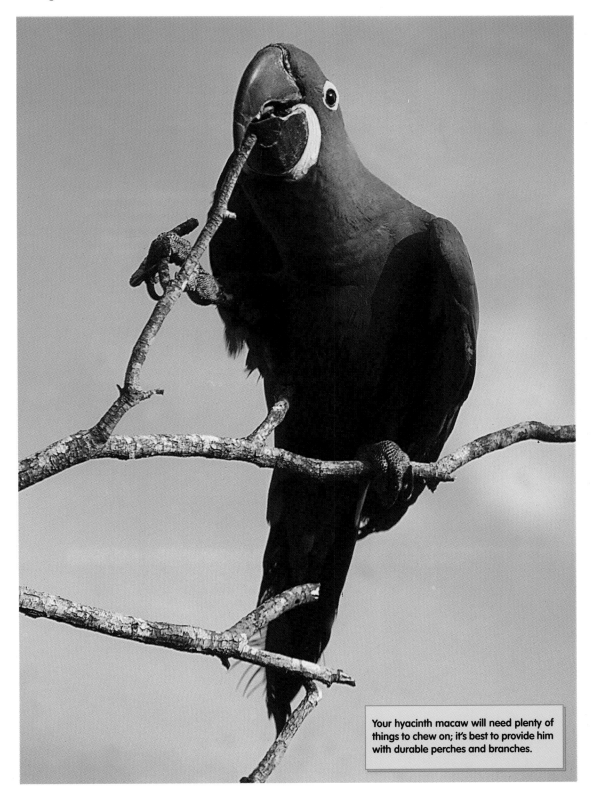

Your hyacinth macaw will need plenty of things to chew on; it's best to provide him with durable perches and branches.

The cage you choose for your macaw should be made of wrought iron or sturdy iron mesh; it should be big enough for the macaw to spread its wings in.

even like to roll in the wet grass. The household bird doesn't have this luxury so you have to compensate for it. One way to solve the problem is to purchase a man-made spray. These sprays are well worth their price because they are not only enjoyed by the birds, but most of the sprays will kill mites as well. You should spray your bird at least once a week. As a precautionary note, be sure to familiarize yourself with any instructions included with the spray before spraying your bird. Some sprays may warn you to avoid getting the spray in your bird's eyes; this may well be a good measure for any spray, especially those designed to rid your bird of mites.

Some macaws also thoroughly enjoy a good bath. However, bathing is not innate behavior and may have to be taught. You can first try placing wet greens in the

perch or playpen for extra exercise. One or more playpens can be set up and connected by ladders near the cage. This will make things easier for the bird that has clipped wings. Playpens can also be placed in other areas of the house for variety, but it is important that they be supplied with food and water in case it is feeding time and the bird is unable to return to its cage. Playpens or perches should be equipped with toys, bells, and other objects the macaw may be interested in. The perch or perches must be made of strong durable wood that is resilient to the macaw's persistent chewing. As with most macaw accessories, a well-built playpen will probably be expensive. Yet all of this should be considered before you purchase your bird. You should not own a large macaw unless you are able to provide for its needs. Remember, a contented pet is a joy to own. Please note that your macaw

will probably destroy a good deal of its toys; try not to be dismayed after buying these things for his amusement.

BATHING

In the wild, macaws delight in bathing in the rain. Some

Macaws love a good bath. Be certain to provide yours with a dish for bathing.

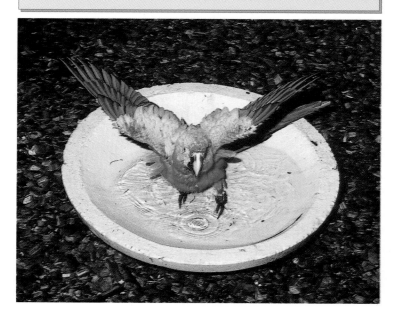

bathing dish, then each time after that add a little water to the dish. Before you know it, the bird will have a full tub and may fully enjoy taking a regular bath. Some bird owners allow their pets to bathe in the kitchen sink; however, if you are not looking, your bird could possibly burn itself under hot water or even drown if the basin is full.

DRAFTS & SUNSHINE

Your pet should live a long active life if you take note of a few precautionary measures. As a concerned macaw owner, one thing you must never do is place your bird's cage directly in front of a window. In doing so, one of two things may occur: the bird will become overheated from too much direct sunlight or it will catch a cold from a draft. Because your bird is living indoors, it does not have the resistance to withstand sudden temperature changes.

If you choose to cover the bird's cage at night, do so consistently, for in time it will come to expect the added insulation provided by the cover and lose some of its natural insulation. Therefore, if the cover is forgotten the bird may catch cold.

Overheating can be just as harmful as a chill. Sunshine is important in moderate doses. The best solution is to place the cage in such a way that the bird can bask in the sun's rays if it chooses to, or avoid the sunlight by stepping to another section of the cage.

CLEANLINESS

The importance of cleanliness in regard to a macaw's well-being cannot be overstressed. Because birds are susceptible to as many diseases as humans, it is imperative that their living quarters are clean at all times. Unlike humans, birds do not recover easily once they have fallen ill, and many disorders are a result of bacterial infections that stem from dirty facilities.

An aviary can provide your macaw with more room than a cage to exercise, play, and even breed in.

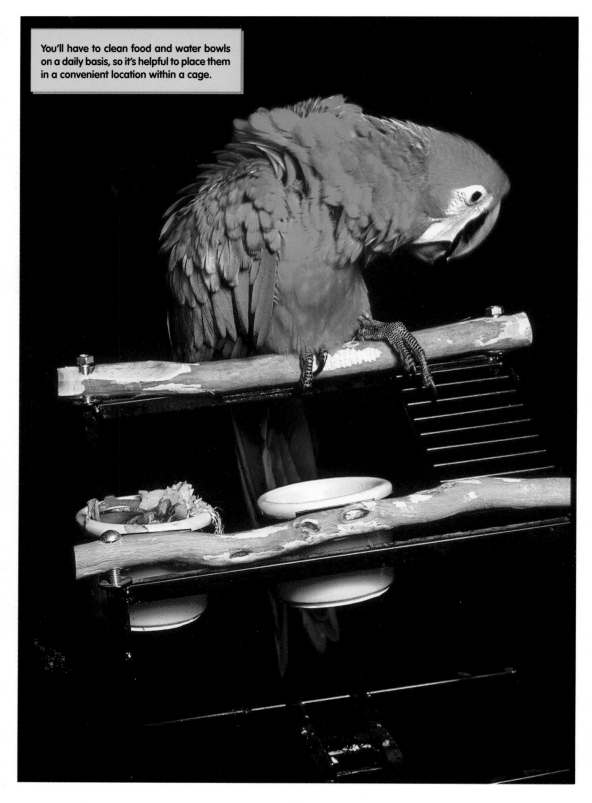

You'll have to clean food and water bowls on a daily basis, so it's helpful to place them in a convenient location within a cage.

Therefore, clean your bird's cage every other day. Scrub the perches, change the gravel, and wash food and water dishes. Make sure fresh food and water are given daily. You should even disinfect the entire cage once a week. Though it would be easier to avoid these chores, your bird will surely suffer from it. You will be rewarded with a healthy and happy pet.

AVIARIES

An outdoor aviary is an excellent enclosure for a macaw to live in. If you have the space and can afford to buy or build a strong aviary, it might be the ideal solution to the housing situation. Aviaries are also the best facilities for breeding purposes.

The size of the aviary is very important. It should be at least 8 feet high, 20 feet long, and 6 or 7 feet wide. These are the best dimensions for the flight space. When someone walks into this area, the bird reacts by flying over him. Therefore, the door to the aviary should be only 4 feet high so the bird won't fly over you and right out the door. A "bird lock" is an even better precautionary measure. You can walk into this small chamber and then lock the door

Two green winged macaws, which are similar to scarlets in coloring, relax on their perch.

Perches now take into account both the function of providing a place for birds to rest and the desire of owners to add colorful good looks to the cage, so they are available in a wide range of colors. Perches are also available with simple screw mechanisms that allow them to be attached firmly without having to extend across the entire width of the cage, saving flight space and cutting down on potentially dangerous obstructions. Photo courtesy of Polly's Pet Products, Inc.

behind you as you proceed to open the door to the flight space. The bird lock will hamper any escape attempts. Macaws are extremely curious and the world beyond their enclosure may seem awfully intriguing to them, so a little prevention certainly can't hurt.

Construction

Aviaries should be constructed of strong, heavy wire mesh. Two-inch hexagonal mesh is recommended for macaws, but this wiring is spacious enough to allow rats, mice, sparrows, and snakes into the aviary. Therefore, it may be necessary to enclose the large wire with smaller mesh to keep intruders out. A two-foot metal strip covering the bottom of the cage will also prevent rats, mice, and snakes from coming in. Sparrows will still be able to

Climbing structures and perches can be made of many types of materials—as long as they are able to withstand the wear and tear of a macaw.

gain entrance if you choose not to use the second layer of wiring.

Floors

There are several types of floors that may be used for aviaries, each with advantages and disadvantages. An earthen floor is obviously the least expensive, but in the long run it may well be costly. A dirt floor is easily contaminated and can cause numerous diseases. Remember that cleanliness is just as important to the aviary bird as it is to the house pet. It is very difficult to keep an earthen floor free from bacteria, and this type of floor also allows easy access for rodents. These unwelcome pests can contaminate a bird's food, frighten breeders from their nests, eat eggs and chicks, and even harm full-grown birds.

Wooden floors are equally inappropriate, because they are hard to maintain, especially when damp, though they do protect against unwelcome visitors.

The best floor is one made of concrete. Though it may be hard on the bird's feet, there are several benefits. Cement floors can be easily cleaned and disinfected, thereby

The blue and gold macaw is highly sociable, easily tamed, and very trusting, making it one of the most popular large parrots.

lessening the chance of disease, and they protect against invaders. You can overcome the problem of harshness to your bird's feet by covering the floor with litter of peat or shredded sugar cane.

SHELTERS

Macaws should be housed in pairs or alone, therefore a shelter need not be excessively large. The shelter should be located at the end of the flight space rather than at the side or middle. The shelter should also be made of concrete, so that the macaw will not destroy it by chewing it to pieces. The concrete should be applied over a wire mesh for durability and sturdiness. The wire mesh will serve as a support for the concrete before it dries as well as for a rough form of the

Although your scarlet might enjoy the company of another macaw, be certain that you have the space for two large birds in your home.

shelter that can be rearranged before the cement is actually mixed or cast. The shelter should be equipped with several high perches. If you plan to leave your bird or birds outdoors all year long, the shelter should be insulated and heated. The insulation should be applied in such a way as to ensure adequate protection for your bird from the elements as well as adequate protection for your bird from himself. Insulating materials can be deadly if ingested by your bird, so care should be used in selecting and applying the material to the shelter. The heating of the shelter can also result in a situation that can be dangerous to your bird. Too much heat, improper electrical fixtures, or exposed wires that the macaw can chew on may prove deadly to your pet.

It would also be a good idea to cover a portion of the flight space to protect against rain and snow. The flight space as well as shelter should have several strong wooden perches. You may also want to give your bird extra wood chips or even a 1-inch by 2-inch stick occasionally to satisfy its chewing needs.

FEEDERS AND WATER CONTAINERS

There are many types of feeders available. Open dishes are frequently used, but macaws enjoy splattering their seed around when it is given to them in open pans. A better feeder is one that has a storage capacity where only a limited amount of food is accessible to the bird. This type saves a lot of waste. Your pet store should have various feeders available for you to choose from.

The best water containers are made of crockery, pottery, or glass, the materials most durable and easiest to clean. Steel and aluminum really don't make satisfactory containers, as they rust and get pitted.

It is strictly up to the owner to decide how to accommodate his macaw. No matter what you decide, always keep in mind the importance of cleanliness, adequate space, and sufficient stimuli. Adherence to this rule should ensure the health and well-being of your pet.

Although some macaws, such as this scarlet, enjoy being with other pets, many will demand your full attention.

Because macaws have such strong beaks and claws, accessories such as feeding dishes should be durable.

Water dishes should be heavy enough that they can't be easily overturned or tipped.

Toys—of all shapes, sizes, and colors—should be provided to your macaw to keep him busy and happy.

Swings and branches can hold your macaw's attention for hours and give him exercise needed for good health.

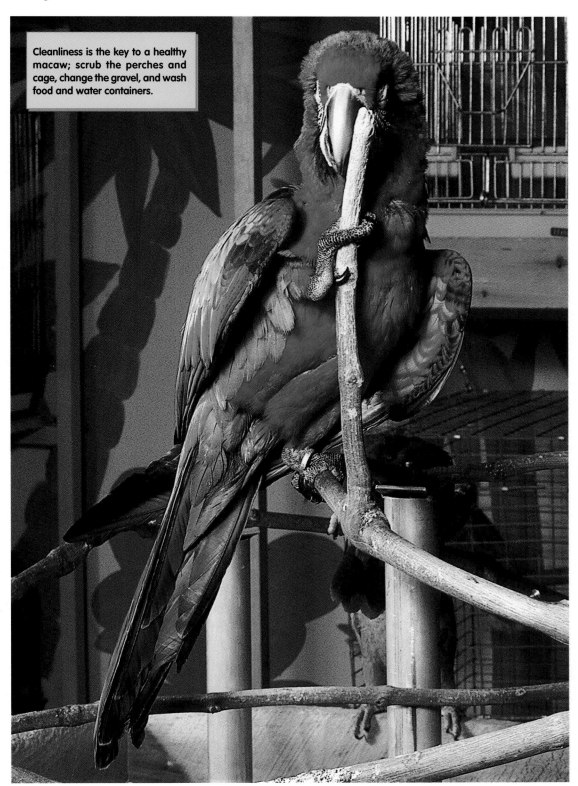

Cleanliness is the key to a healthy macaw; scrub the perches and cage, change the gravel, and wash food and water containers.

Feeding Your Macaw

A proper diet is essential in order to ensure that your macaw has a long and healthy life in captivity. It is not necessary to try and duplicate the type of diet a macaw is accustomed to in the wild. In fact, to do so might even prove harmful to the pet bird.

In the wild, macaws eat a good deal of nuts, seeds from trees, and many fruits, all of which are quite high in calories. Because macaws are very active in their native lands, there is a greater need for extra calories. In captivity, however, the opposite is true. Domestic birds are a lot less active and therefore have trouble burning off calories. If they are given too many rich foods, they will soon become fat and lazy. Yet because caged macaws prefer these foods and will eat them continuously if allowed to do so, it is the owner's responsibility to make sure his pet is not overly indulged.

Macaws are like people in that they all develop individual tastes. However, the similarities end there. Macaws are creatures of habit. They want and expect the same meal day in and day out. They are not the least bit interested in trying something new and

Like birds in the wild, domestic macaws require a variety of nuts, seeds, and fruits for a complete diet.

different. In fact, they often refuse any change of diet. A special treat (a slice of apple, a dab of peanut butter) is perhaps the only exception. Macaws thrive on routine; therefore it is best to feed, water, and clean at the same time each day. Any change in routine is apt make your bird

nervous and suspicious. It is also advisable to keep the same water and feed dishes for as long as possible. Though changing containers probably won't create any serious problems, it might cause your bird to go off its feed for a few days.

Pet macaws should have a diet that is high in protein. Sunflower seeds are a commonly used macaw food. But because they are rich in fats, if fed to your macaw exclusively the bird will become fat, its beak and claws overgrown and its plumage dull. Mineral and vitamin deficiencies may also develop. Therefore, it is essential that your macaw be given a well-rounded diet. Such a diet would consist of a good parrot mix (preferably bagged, not boxed, to stay fresher), health grit, cuttlebone or lava stone, greenfood, and a dietary supplement. Pumpkin seeds, raw unsalted peanuts, safflower, pigeon feed, brewers yeast pellets, and a small

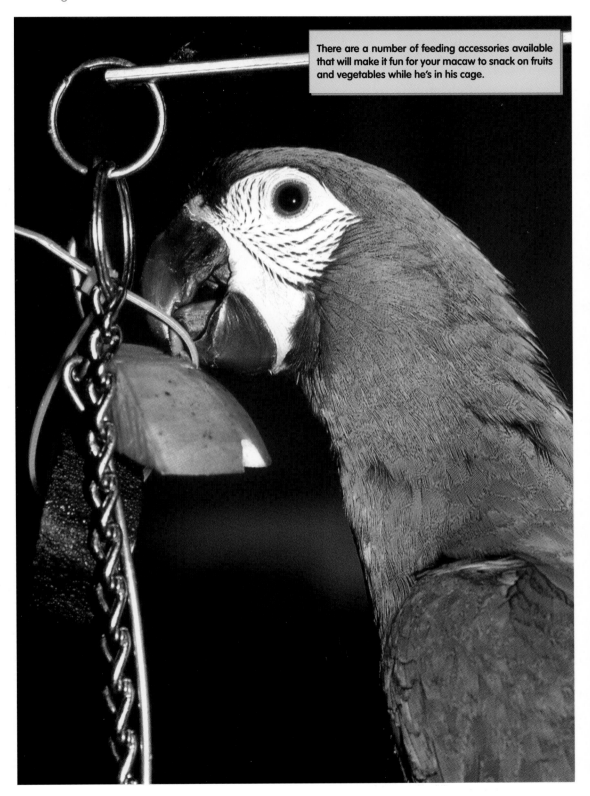

There are a number of feeding accessories available that will make it fun for your macaw to snack on fruits and vegetables while he's in his cage.

One of the best ways to make sure that bird treats really appeal to birds' tastes is to put plenty of bird-pleasing exotic fruits and nuts into them. Some treats contain real papaya, coconut, pineapple, and red peppers, in addition to other nutritious vegetables. Photo courtesy of Sun Seed Company.

portion of good dry kibble dog food also add to a well-balanced diet.

All macaws must have gravel or health grit added to their diet, both of which serve a dual purpose. First and foremost, because birds have no teeth to chew their food, the gravel or grit helps to

Complement the fresh foods you prepare for your macaw with parrot mixes and dry kibble dog food.

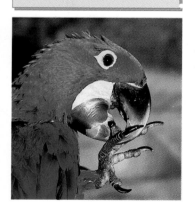

grind seeds up in the bird's gizzard. Second, they furnish the bird with several important minerals that may be missing in their other foods. It is wise to purchase a prepared grit from a pet shop; ordinary sand or gravel is a poor substitute and may even be dangerous to your bird's health.

Cuttlebone helps to keep a bird's beak trim, and it also provides needed calcium and salt. Because many macaws will destroy a cuttlebone just seconds after it is offered to them, some macaw owners give their pets lava stone, which is larger, tougher, and serves the same purpose.

Greenfoods should be given sparingly, because they often cause diarrhea. Lettuce has little nutritional value and should not be fed to your pet. Carrot tops and dandelions are much more nutritious, as well as watercress, green peas in the pod, celery, carrots, ripe tomato, and corn on the cob.

Dietary supplements consist of liquid vitamins that

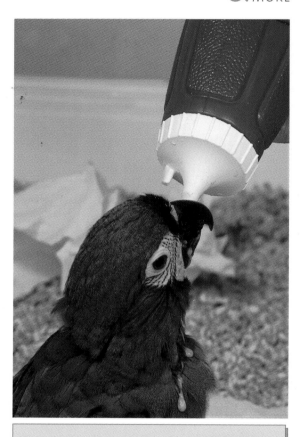

One way you can provide your young macaw with nourishment is to hand-feed it a soft food mash using a small squeeze bottle.

dissolve in water. They should be given daily.

Fruits, like greens, can cause diarrhea, but they are an acceptable food source if given in small quantities. Macaws enjoy a bit of orange, apple, banana, soaked raisins, and a few grapes. They also like Brazil nuts and large dog biscuits as a special treat.

Your pet should always be provided with fresh, cool water. Water dishes should be cleaned daily to protect against infectious bacteria. If you follow the diet as it is given here, your macaw should remain healthy and content for many years.

It's important that your macaw's food dishes be cleaned daily to prevent food from spoiling and spreading bacteria.

Many owners prefer to feed their young macaws with a syringe that has had the needle removed.

Taming and Training

Patience, love, and understanding are the key ingredients needed to successfully tame and eventually train a macaw. Given the proper attention, a macaw can be as loving and gentle as any pet dog. By the same token, if this highly intelligent animal is mistreated or frightened during training, it can become extremely vicious. Because a macaw has a powerful beak and grasping claws, you could very well find yourself in a dangerous situation. Though you should not feel

intimidated by your pet, it is important to approach it cautiously and as confidently as possible. A bird can easily detect human fear and will then become frightened itself. A fear biter is as potentially dangerous as a vicious bird.

As previously mentioned, macaws have very distinct personalities. You may find that you have purchased a naturally nasty bird. There is a chance that you will eventually be able to gain the bird's trust, but some macaws will never become gentle. You may then have to decide if it

is wise to keep the bird in your home.

Before you begin taming your macaw, it is important to remember that you must never punish your pet, for though the macaw is intelligent, it does not have the mentality to comprehend why it is being punished. In the past some bird owners would rap their parrots over the head if they misbehaved. Having no idea why they were being so unjustly treated, the birds became frightened and nasty. If you love your bird and treat it kindly it is likely

You'll have the best results taming and training your macaw if you are patient and kind with him.

Some birds may become overconfident if allowed to ride on your shoulder. Keeping the bird at eye level with you or lower should remind him who's boss.

Toys can be used during training to make things fun and enjoyable for both you and your macaw.

It may take some time and practice to get used to hand taming, but the work leads to great results.

If given the chance, your macaw will chew on anything! This severe macaw is enjoying a dog bone.

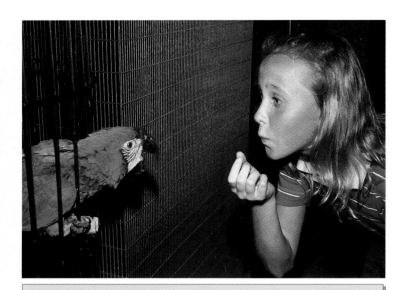

Gaining your bird's trust is the first step in taming him; start by approaching his cage frequently.

within the security of its home. However, if something should alarm your bird and it flies away, it will become hopelessly lost.

Wing clipping is perfectly painless if done correctly. There are several ways of going about it. Some experts like to clip the primary flight feathers on both wings to give the bird a balanced look. Others prefer to clip all primary flight feathers on just one wing. This method is often preferred because the bird abandons all efforts to fly. When a bird tries to fly with a clipped wing it never reaches its intended goal, as it flies in a curve. After a few more attempts, the bird gets discouraged and gives up altogether.

Wings should only be clipped by those who know what they are doing. Feathers should not be cut closer than the primary coverts to allow room for a quill that might

to reciprocate in the same fashion.

Before you attempt to tame your bird, it is essential that you gain its trust. Begin by placing the bird's cage in an area where there is a lot of human activity. The family room would be ideal. Macaws are naturally curious and will enjoy all the goings-on. Approach the cage frequently, talking quietly to your bird. Sudden gestures or noises will upset your new arrival, so try to minimize distractions. In short order the bird should adapt to its human environment.

WING CLIPPING

Though wing clipping may seem cruel to some, it is really quite harmless. It may, in fact, spare you and your pet needless stress. If a bird escapes during the initial period of taming it can become traumatized while you attempt to recapture it. All progress you have made to

this point may be lost. Recapturing a frightened macaw is no fun for you, either. Even a completely tame bird might escape if frightened. Usually a macaw is perfectly content to stay

Wing clipping, a harmless and painless procedure, will prevent your bird from escaping during training.

As soon as you and your new bird become acquainted you can teach him to step onto a stick.

split. An ingrown feather can result from a quill that has split down into the feather follicle.

HAND TAMING

Within a few days, your bird should be acquainted enough with its new home to begin hand taming. To wait any longer than a week only wastes time and may hinder the process. Remember that careful and confident movements are essential at this time. Approach your bird slowly and quietly. Offer it some tidbit of food—a piece of apple or banana would be fine. Always talk to it reassuringly. Because you have taken away the bird's ability to fly, the only means it has left to protect itself is its beak. A young macaw will only bite if it is afraid. Remove the need for fear and you will have won half the battle.

After the bird appears to have accepted you, hold a stick (one the size of a shortened broom handle would be best) up to its chest.

Most often the bird will step onto it. If it does not, a little gentle pressure just above its legs usually guarantees results. However, do not force your bird to perform. If it really objects, quit and try again later. If all is going well, the bird will grab the stick with its beak and climb onto it. You must realize that the bird is not trying to bite you; rather, it is assessing the safety of this new perch by holding it firmly in its beak.

When you have gone through this routine a few times successfully, use your free hand to hold the bird's attention as you edge it over to the hand holding the perch. Once the macaw is on your hand, remove the perch. If you have done this properly, your bird probably won't realize he's on your hand if you remain calm and steady. When you feel it is safe to do so, walk around the room with the bird on your hand. He will be confused, but he'll realize that so far no harm has come to him and he should remain quietly on your hand. Continue to reassure it by talking softly and offering a few more tidbits. This first session is very important. If all has gone well by the time you place the bird back in its cage, future sessions should run smoothly.

In the second session you should handle the bird in basically the same fashion, only this

It's important to begin training early—an untamed macaw may use its powerful beak when threatened or alarmed.

time do away with the perch. Repeated use of the perch will result in a macaw that is totally stick trained. This is not desirable because there will always be a barrier between you and your pet. From this point forward only offer your hand or arm as a perch. In a short time the bird will probably enjoy a ride on your shoulder. By now you and your bird will have established a trusting relationship. The bird should have no reason to bite you. If

Treat sticks specially formulated for large hookbills and containing real fruits, nuts, and vegetables are widely available—they even have different flavorings to vary the taste appeal. Photo courtesy of Sun Seed Company.

it should attempt to snap at your fingers, quickly turn your wrist toward you, pulling the finger away. At the same time gently push the macaw's chin with another finger to misguide its aim. Be patient and kind and soon the nipping behavior should subside.

After a macaw is completely hand tamed it can be trained to perform endless tricks. By observing the bird's natural behavior and using a little imagination, a macaw can be taught to play with toys, ring bells, and do somersaults.

Once your macaw is comfortably perched on the stick, gradually ease him onto your hand.

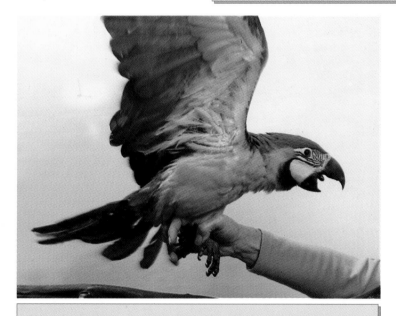

Hold your arm steady and remove the perch, then give your macaw a moment or two to calm down.

are several ways to teach a macaw to talk, and as long as you use one of them consistently, you should be successful.

One of the most popular methods used is a bird training record. The same word, phrase, or phrases are repeated continuously. Meanwhile, you are at liberty to leave the bird and the monotony of the record's repetition. Though most of the training records on the market are devised for

After your macaw feels secure on your arm, begin to walk slowly around the room.

TALKING

Macaws are not noted for their talking ability. However, there is always an exception to the rule, and almost any macaw can learn to say a few words if you devote enough time to training it. A younger bird will become a better talker, as will a tamer bird.

The key factor in teaching a macaw to talk is "repetition." Remember, as intelligent as a macaw appears to be, it is really only a mimic. It must hear the same word over and over again in order to learn how to repeat it. Macaws can not associate spoken words with their meanings. There parakeets, they work just fine for macaws. The best records to buy have one or two simple phrases on both sides, spoken in a clear and concise feminine voice. For some reason parrots find it easier to mimic female voices than male voices, though some birds mimic both equally well. After your bird has listened to the record for awhile, you should begin repeating the words to yourself. That way the bird will learn to respond to you instead of the record. The first word is always the hardest to learn, but it is usually easier after that. One drawback with this method is that you might not like the phrases selected for the record. You might in that case make a tape recording of your own voice and the words you choose the bird to learn. The principle is basically the same.

Another training method is a daily lesson routine between

The training process is well worth the effort because it will help you establish a trusting relationship with your macaw.

Once hand tamed, a macaw can be trained to play with toys and perform tricks.

owner and pet. Set aside 20 minutes each day to work with your bird. Two 20-minute sessions a day would be better but are not necessary. Choose a simple phrase and repeat it slowly over and over again. It is important that these sessions be held at the same time every day. Remember, macaws thrive on routine.

While training, some people like to cover the bird's cage to avoid distractions. This works well with some birds; others have a tendency to fall asleep. Some experts suggest having the bird perch on the trainer's hand, facing his mouth. This way the trainer has the bird's undivided attention.

It may take months before a macaw utters its first word, so be patient. Don't expect too much from your pet. After the first word has been spoken, the rest will come much easier. Once a macaw has developed a strong attachment for its human family, almost anything is possible.

Breeding Macaws

Though the breeding season for macaws is in the spring, it is best to allow the prospective parents to become well acquainted before then. This process in itself may take awhile. Sometimes when a chosen cock and hen meet for the first time, they are completely taken with each other and will probably become good mates. Other pairs turn the aviary into a battleground. Don't be foolish enough to think this first encounter is merely a lover's quarrel and will work itself out. It won't! Separate the birds immediately before one of them is injured or even killed. Other birds become neither friend nor foe; they are simply indifferent. Remember that even if a pair gets along well, you may find as time goes on that they have no intentions of rearing a family. This could well be because the birds are of the same sex. Many dismayed bird fanciers have run into this very problem. In this respect, Dr. Vriends's chart may help.

SEXING MACAWS
Hyacinth Macaw—sexes are alike, but the hen is usually smaller.
Scarlet Macaw—sexes are alike, but female is smaller with shorter and less hooked bill.
Green Winged Macaw—sexes are alike, but female has a shorter and broader bill

Breeding will not be successful unless a pair of macaws is compatible and they become good mates.

A pair of breeding blue and gold macaws will need plenty of privacy during the breeding period.

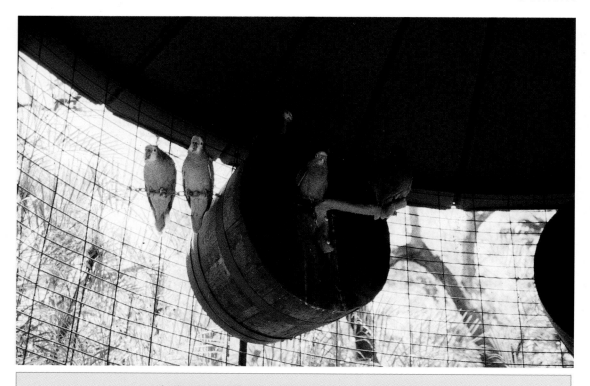

A properly placed nesting box is an essential component of breeding success.

with a more arched culmen. (The culmen is the uppermost edge of the bill).

Illiger's Macaw—sexes are alike, but female has less red on the forehead (this is not always reliable, as red may vary in individual birds of either sex).

Noble Macaw—sexes are alike, but female somewhat smaller.

Red-Bellied Macaw—sexes are alike, but female is smaller.

If you have several macaws, perhaps the best way to pair them is through natural selection, which will allow the birds to choose their own mates. Place all the birds in an aviary and wait until they select partners. After this has been accomplished, keep the pairs in separate partners.

Then keep the pairs in separate aviaries, as most macaws will not appreciate company at this time.

When you are satisfied that you are working with a good pair of breeders (though you will never be completely sure of this) it is time to get them started on a good diet that will

> Some pairs just won't get along— no matter how much time you give them to become a pair.

last through the breeding season. If you plan to have the birds feed their young they must have a diet consisting of various foods. Aside from the diet described in the chapter on feeding, you might add some whole wheat bread, corn on the cob, soaked grain, and wheat germ oil.

Probably the most important factor in successful breeding is the size and location of the nesting box. It is a simple fact that macaws will reject the box if they aren't pleased with it. These birds like to nest on the ground in long, low boxes. The box should be at least 5 or 6 feet long, 3 or 4 feet wide and 2 feet high. Because macaws love to chew and can do considerable damage, some people choose to use a hollow

Breeding birds can be labor intensive and time consuming, but the results are well worth it.

It takes many weeks for feathers and true colors to develop on chicks, like those on these young military and blue and gold macaws.

tree trunk or an old barrel for the nesting box. The entrance to any of these nesting quarters should be large enough for the birds to enter and exit with ease. More than one box per pair is advisable to give the birds a choice.

It is important that the box be securely fastened so it won't move around and alarm the occupants. The bottom should be slightly slanted toward the back to keep the eggs from rolling about. The floor should also be covered with wood shavings. These shavings should be moistened because macaws are accustomed to humidity in the wild.

A dry atmosphere may harden the egg's membrane, making it difficult for the chick to peck out at hatching time.

Birds are picky about their nesting quarters. If they reject their box, try moving it to another area of the flight space. Macaws usually have a sound reason for not accepting the nesting box. It may be because they feel it is in a draft or too close to birds in another aviary. Whatever the reason, it's best to do what you can to make sure they are content.

Another consideration is the temperature in their cage. Outdoor birds may need added heat to ward off chill. A heat bulb should solve this problem.

Remember, once the hen lays her egg don't intrude on her privacy more than is necessary. Macaws are very protective during the breeding season and may be hostile toward you. Or, if they are thoroughly annoyed by human interference, they may abandon the nest. If all goes well, the hen will lay two or three shiny white eggs. The chicks will appear in 23 to 24 days.

Macaws usually tolerate their young for a long while after they leave the nest. However, if you choose to hand raise the baby birds, it's best to take them from their mother before they are old enough to venture out on their own.

Breeding and raising macaws is a very time-consuming project that requires a great deal of patience on your part. Try to keep this in mind when all your efforts seem to have been in vain. Successful breeding may take years, but the end result is well worth the wait.

Birds chosen for mating must be of suitable age; macaws generally do not mate before their fifth year.

When determining the sex of red-bellied macaws, note that the sexes are generally alike, but the females are smaller.

A pair of Illiger's macaws preen each other, an act that reinforces the bond between two birds.

A two-day-old blue and gold macaw.

Though he's not yet as handsome as his adult counterparts, this one-month-old hyacinth chick is already showing signs of striking coloring.

Have some patience if it's not "love at first sight" with your macaws. Breeding success may take time.

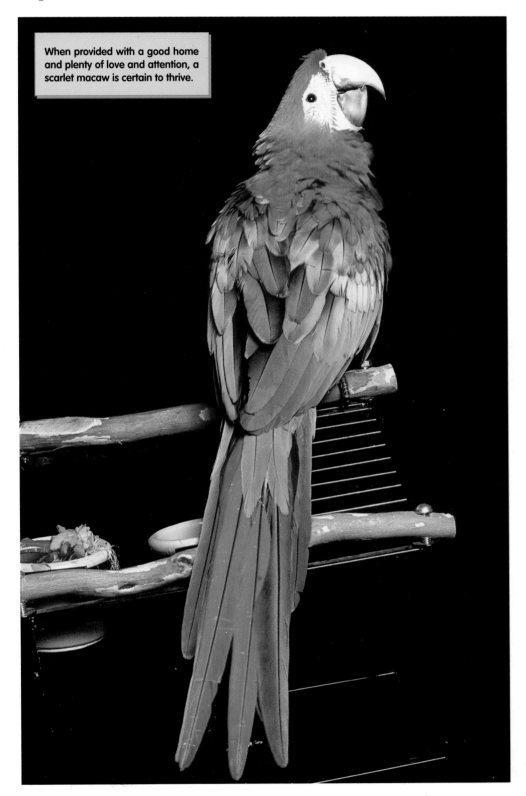

When provided with a good home and plenty of love and attention, a scarlet macaw is certain to thrive.

Your Macaw's Good Health

Unfortunately, macaws are susceptible to many disorders. No matter how hard you try to keep your pet in good health, the possibility of it becoming ill always exists. It is important to spot a disease in its early stages in order to promptly administer medication. If a disease progresses unattended, chances of recovery are very poor. Because relatively little is known of macaw ailments and their cures, early diagnosis and treatment are essential.

The following is a discussion of various diseases and ailments your macaw might contract. Although preliminary treatment can be prescribed for all of them, you should consult a veterinarian if symptoms persist.

COLDS

A macaw catches a cold in much the same way humans do, as a result of viral infection aided by chill and draft. Unfortunately, a cold can be more serious for a bird because it might easily develop into pneumonia.

Symptoms of this disorder are typical: runny nose, sneezing, coughing, watery eyes, listlessness, lack of appetite, and possibly diarrhea. The bird will probably stand with two feet on the perch, its head tucked under a wing on its back, and its feathers puffed up. Its

Diseases and viruses can spread rapidly throughout a collection of birds; watch your birds carefully to monitor their health.

It's easier to treat an ill bird if it is isolated from the others; the bird will also be able to concentrate its energy on recuperation.

nostrils may become clogged with hardening discharge. In short, your bird will look and feel miserable. This condition slowly weakens the bird's resistance.

If you have other birds, it is best to isolate the sick bird. Although colds are contagious to other birds, you are unable to catch the virus from your pet. Keep the bird in a very warm environment of at least 80° to 85° F. If the bird seems to be mildly infected, you can try adding a saline laxative to its drinking water for the first 24 hours. Meanwhile, wipe its nostrils with a light antiseptic every day until the discharge has cleared up. In addition, you should add 25 to 50

milligrams of terramycin or aureomycin to 2 ounces of water for about three or four days. If symptoms persist, you should take your bird to a veterinarian for added treatment. Not all vets are knowledgeable when it comes to birds, so make sure you visit one that is familiar with bird diseases and ailments.

PNEUMONIA

Pneumonia often develops as a result of a prolonged cold or if a bird has withstood too much heat or too much cold. A great deal of excess fluid builds up in the bird's lungs, causing them to become very spongy as well as watery.

If a young bird catches pneumonia it can usually recover, but it will always remain frail and susceptible to various diseases throughout its life.

Treatment for this ailment is similar to that for a cold. However, it is essential to administer an antibiotic; aureomycin, terramycin, or achromycin is recommended.

If your macaw is extremely ill, it may be impossible to administer medication orally. Consult your veterinarian, as medication may have to be given through injection.

PSITTACOSIS

Psittacosis, though a rarity, has caused a public uproar in

A healthy bird will have bright clear eyes and a smooth beak.

As with many caged birds, supplementing your macaw's diet with cuttlebone will help ensure good health.

Probably the first symptom you will notice is small mounds on the bird's head or just above its eyes. These mounds are actually lumps of hardened mucus that have accumulated behind clogged sinus passages. The mounds are usually yellow and tend to have a cheese-like consistency. Other symptoms are swollen eyes (sometimes forced shut) and puffy sacs under the eyes.

The best way to relieve the bird is to first drain the mounds so as not to injure any tissue. Proper drainage should actually be done with minor surgery, pricking the mound with a sterilized pin. In a few days a scab will form.

Massage the scab slightly to remove it. Do the best you can to remove all the cheese-like material so that the condition will not recur. Then cleanse the area with a mild disinfectant.

In order to clear swollen eyes and eye sacs, gently apply yellow oxide of mercury ointment for three or four days.

ASTHMA

Asthma is also brought on by the aftermath of a cold. Though it is a low-grade infection, it may have to be treated for up to six months. If your bird has just recuperated from a cold but continues to have trouble

past years because it is transmissible to humans. It is commonly known as "parrot fever." However, with the help of modern medicine, this disease can be controlled. Symptoms are similar to a severe cold or pneumonia. Antibiotics are used to combat the bacteria (actually a rickettsia). It is sometimes necessary to take a blood sample to accurately diagnose psittacosis.

Chances of your macaw contracting this bacteria are very slim. However, if you have sufficient reason to suspect that your bird is indeed afflicted with the disease, it would be best to have a blood test taken. Because a macaw is a large bird, the test should not prove harmful to him.

SINUS PROBLEMS

Sinus trouble is a low-grade infection usually brought on by the aftermath of a cold.

You can trust that your bird is being fed the most thoroughly researched formulation available. Look for a new handfeeding formula, which is coming out soon. Photo courtesy of Roudybush.

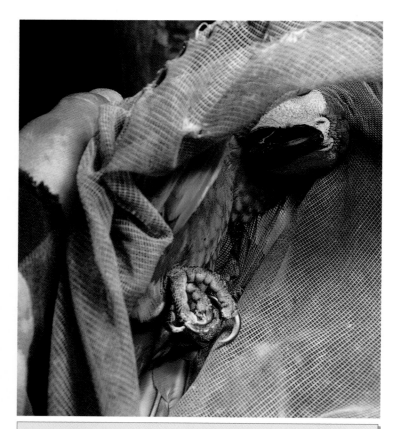

It may be necessary to wrap your macaw in a cloth when examining him for mites or other health problems.

and eliminate the trouble by administering the proper laxative; an oily laxative is helpful in most cases.

NAUSEA

Macaws will regurgitate for several reasons. It usually means they have a desire to mate. They will purposely bring up their food to offer to their mate. If a bird lives alone it might bestow this customary honor upon you. Try not to be discouraged or alarmed, for its odd behavior will pass quickly enough.

However, if the bird continues to vomit, it may be a sign of some disorder. Nausea is often associated with crop ailments including sour crop, crop impaction, and molds. These maladies can be treated with antibiotics.

GOING-LIGHT

Going-light refers to loss of weight. It is actually a

Overgrown claws may be carefully clipped, but it's best to avoid the problem in the first place.

breathing and makes a pathetic wheezing sound, it probably has asthma.

The best way to combat this ailment is to isolate the bird and administer an inhalant every day for an hour. Though this may seem like a slow way to cure the infection, it often has the best results. Antibiotics have proved ineffective for treatment of asthma.

DIARRHEA

Diarrhea, as previously mentioned, is actually a symptom of other disorders and may also be caused by a change of diet. Diarrhea can be fatal if left unattended.

Certain medicines are prescribed for treatment, but some may be too harsh. Many owners recommend Kaopectate®, which can be given every three hours. If your bird has bloody diarrhea do not administer any type of medicine, because it will only worsen the problem. In such a case it is best to call upon a veterinarian.

CONSTIPATION

Constipation is usually caused by colds or the presence of worms or mites in the bird's system. When a bird is constipated, its droppings will be white. You can clear the digestive tract symptom rather than a disease. Going-light occurs when a bird has a high metabolic rate and needs to constantly make up for spent energy. When a parrot isn't feeling well it often goes off its diet, using its flesh for nourishment as a result. This, of course, can lead to rapid weight loss. This condition can also be fatal if the cause of the trouble is not found and treated.

MOLDS

Fungi are responsible for many illnesses in pet birds. Fungus molds can be contracted in numerous ways. Dirty water, rotten seeds, moldy food, dampness, and filth all cause molds. Treatment varies depending on the type and location of the infection. Unfortunately, most treatments are unsuccessful. The best way to combat the problem is to prevent it altogether. Clean and disinfect the bird's living quarters frequently!

If your bird does develop a mold, it can affect many different parts of its body. Symptoms that resemble those of a cold are caused by molds in the mouth. Others affect the digestive tract and cause diarrhea. Some molds draw water from the bird, causing the bird's body to actually become mushy.

Copper sulfate is one remedy that often has the best results in treating molds if administered in diluted form. If your bird has an

A bird that sits with its feathers fluffed up or its head tucked under a wing may be ill.

external mold, keep him in a warm room and clean the infected area with a mild disinfectant. Then apply a mild astringent.

Sprays are available that will help with your bird's mite problems—your macaw will love the attention, too.

Feather plucking, a serious and difficult habit to break, can be the result of a bird's frustration or a deficiency in its diet.

BACTERIAL AND PROTOZOAN ENTERITIS

Enteritis is a deadly disease often contracted by aviary birds. It is caused by overcrowded and dirty living quarters. Again, a macaw living in filth is doomed. Your charges ask so little of you and give so much in return, they shouldn't have to suffer needlessly.

Symptoms of enteritis are diarrhea, weight loss, weakness, and listlessness. The disease spreads quickly and can cause rapid death. Treat with aureomycin.

FRENCH MOLT

Though macaws naturally molt (lose and grow new feathers) twice a year, continued feather loss and replacement is unhealthy. Birds with French molt are weak because the constant replacement of feathers takes all their strength. Most often, birds suffering from this ailment look ruffled and are unable to fly.

Though the actual cause of French molt is unknown, many attribute it to either dietary deficiencies or mites. The best prevention is to spray your bird frequently to protect against mites and make sure you are feeding him a well-rounded diet.

FEATHER PLUCKING

Birds pull their feathers out because they are frustrated or because they are suffering from a dietary deficiency. If your bird plucks his feathers but lives in an environment rich with stimuli and you pay a good deal of attention to him, chances are something is lacking in his diet. You can remedy the situation by adding a dietary supplement (liquid vitamins are recommended) to its diet. See the chapter on feeding for further discussion of proper diet.

If your bird eats well, then perhaps it is bored. You can break its feather plucking habit by paying more attention to it and buying it more toys so it can amuse itself while you're away.

MITES

Red mites are most common in aviary birds. They seem to attack hens and

Overgrown claws may be carefully trimmed with clippers, like those used for dogs.

nesting birds most often and actually suck their blood. If the aviary is heavily infested with red mites, they can cause the deaths of their victims. Inspect for mites in corners, cracks, and behind nest boxes. These tiny pests are difficult to get rid of. The best solution is to spray cages once a week.

Feather and quill mites can destroy a bird's plumage. If feathers appear ratty or chewed up, there is good reason to suspect feather mites as the cause. Spray your bird or birds with a mild insecticide.

Scaly leg mites attack the bird's legs, often causing inflammation. You can treat your pet by applying mite oil or salve directly on the infected areas. This should suffocate the mites and soothe inflammation.

OVERGROWN BEAK AND CLAWS

The beak and claws of a macaw grow in much the same way as our fingernails, at a fairly regular rate. Overgrowth can be attributed to a lack of material to chew on and perches that are too small to allow the bird to use its claws sufficiently.

If a beak becomes overgrown, it will have to be trimmed. This is not going to be an easy task with a macaw

Have some styptic powder handy in case you mistakenly cut into the blood vessel of the bird's claw.

because you will have difficulty restraining it. It would be best if you had a partner to help you, then one of you could hold the bird while the other proceeds to trim its beak. A dog toenail clipper will be the best tool for the task. If you should accidentally cut the vein in the beak, apply iron sulfate or hydrogen peroxide to stop the bleeding.

You can wear down overgrown claws by applying

sand to the bottom of a perch (select a larger perch than the bird has been using) by painting it on with shellac. Overgrown claws and beaks are obviously due to neglect. Please take precautions in the future so that they won't recur.

EGG-BINDING

Egg-binding can be very a serious condition if not detected and treated right away. It occurs when an egg gets caught in the oviduct. Occasionally, even female birds that are not used for breeding lay eggs are afflicted. Symptoms are ruffled feathers, loss of spirit, obvious weakness, and straining gestures to remove the egg.

Treat the bird by placing it in a warm environment. The temperature should range between 80° and 85° F. Administer a bit of olive oil to the vent and massage the area very gently. Normally the egg will be laid within the next few hours.

Many bird owners prefer to trim their bird's overgrown nails by grinding them.

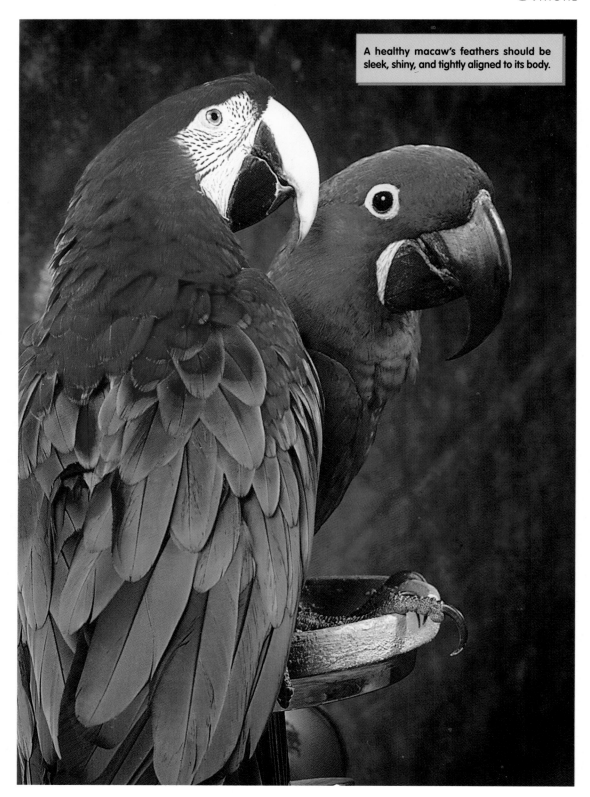

A healthy macaw's feathers should be sleek, shiny, and tightly aligned to its body.

Lack of proper diet and exercise causes egg-binding, which—as you should realize by now—can easily be avoided.

TUMORS

Old macaws are more likely to have tumors than younger birds. Lipomas are benign fatty tumors that can be removed by surgery. Consult a veterinarian with the knowledge and proper equipment for this type of operation. Lipomas are usually found on the chest and occasionally on the bird's wings. Tumors on the wings are very painful because they sometimes grow so large the bird can't fold its wing properly. These can also be removed with surgery.

Not all tumors are benign. Many are cancerous and cannot be cured. These are often internal and impossible to detect.

ARTHRITIS

Arthritis is also seen in older parrots. Though no one is sure of its cause, many believe arthritis is a result of improper diet. Unfortunately, once a bird is afflicted with arthritis there is no cure.

Exercise is an important part of a bird's health regime.

Again, adequate diet and exercise will save your pet from unnecessary suffering.

The treatments described in this chapter for various ailments are not always successful; however, they are responsible for a high rate of recovery. The best medication for your pet bird is prevention; a good percentage of diseases and ailments are a direct result of neglect. If you are a responsible pet owner and care for your bird in the manner described throughout this book, chances are your pet will live a long and healthy life.

A little prevention goes a long way when it comes to your bird's good health. Proper care will ensure that the two of you will spend many years together.

A healthy and happy bird is a joy to own.

Be certain that the macaw you select—whether it be a severe, scarlet, hyacinth, or blue and gold—is the right species for you and your family.

Selecting the
Right Macaw

THE LARGER MACAWS

Hyacinth Macaw

The hyacinth macaw, *Anodorhynchus hyacinthinus* (Latham), is the largest member of the entire parrot family. It is nearly three feet long, with a large and powerful black beak. The overall coloring of the hyacinth is a lustrous cobalt blue. Its wings and tail are an even deeper shade of the same color. This species has a bright yellow ring around its eyes and along the sides of the lower part of its beak.

The hyacinth is a native of central Brazil, south of the Amazon River. It lives in the buriti palm tree, which can be found in swamps surrounding lakes and rivers. Less social than most other macaws, this species is usually only seen in pairs. On occasion they are encountered in groups of five, which are probably family units. The hyacinth nests in the hollows of tree trunks or sometimes in cliffs, and the female lays three eggs. Little else is known of these magnificent beauties in their wild state.

In captivity these birds soon grow tame and are exceptionally affectionate, but

The striking cobalt-blue color of the hyacinth macaw contrasts sharply with the birds' bare yellow cheek patch.

owing to their enormous size they are not suitable pets for the average bird fancier. Also, because the hyacinth is rare it is one of the most expensive macaws to purchase. For that matter, they are seldom offered for sale.

For those who do choose to own a hyacinth, there are only two suitable living accommodations: a very large made-to-order iron cage or a strong aviary. Why all the precaution? The hyacinth can snap off the end of a broom as easily as if it were a matchstick. That's 300 pounds of biting pressure per square inch! It should be easy to guess what this bird is capable of doing to an average cage! Hyacinths also like to gnaw on wood, which explains why they should be kept in an iron cage.

The hyacinth is very hardy, though awkward and clumsy due to its enormous size. However, they can practically destroy their perches with their incessant gnawing, so remember to replace perches frequently. This may seem to be a bit of a bother, but keep in mind that gnawing is essential to keep the beak in good condition and to prevent its overgrowth.

Like other macaws, hyacinths love to snack on nuts and other treats.

Also, one should supply the hyacinth with green bark, foliage, and fresh branches daily for gnawing. During the winter, the hyacinth should be provided with a shelter that is slightly heated.

The hyacinth was first bred in captivity in Illinois in 1971, by R.C. Small.

Blue and Gold Macaw

The blue and gold macaw, *Ara ararauna* (Linnaeus), also known as the blue and yellow, is one of the larger macaws. The cock grows to a length of approximately 34 inches; the hen is slightly smaller. The tail, wings, back, and neck of the blue and gold are a bright, almost turquoise, blue. Its forehead and crown are a greenish blue. Deep golden yellow dominates its undersides except for a bluish yellow on the underparts of its tail and a black collar just beneath its face. Its cheek patch is white lined with a trace of black feathers. Beak and feet are totally black. The eyes can be either bright or pale yellow. Plumage is similar in both sexes.

This species can be found in the jungles of Panama and Columbia, as well as in parts of Brazil, Venezuela, Ecuador, and Peru. This suggests that the blue and gold is more adaptable to various environments in comparison to other macaws that are only found in localized areas.

In the wild, the hen will usually lay two glossy white eggs and hatch them on her own. The young birds will emerge between 23 and 24 days, although in captivity incubation time is between 25 and 28 days. They will remain in the nest until they are three months old, by which time they will have attained their full plumage.

In captivity the blue and gold will often nest and hatch young, but it usually takes a long time. It may even take years to breed successfully because it may be difficult to match two birds that will nest. And though it may sound silly, even if you bought two macaws for breeding purposes, guaranteed mates, they could very well turn out to be of the same sex. It does happen.

For those of you who wish to try breeding this species, a large hollow tree trunk or an old barrel with a round opening should be provided as a nesting box for the hen. The box should be 40 inches long, 2 feet wide and 32 inches high. The entrance can be either 10 inches square or 10 inches in diameter. The floor of the nesting box should be slightly slanted toward the back so that the eggs won't roll out. Macaws should be provided with a nest box all year because they will want to roost there. If you decide to breed, keep in mind that even the gentlest macaw will be very protective at this time and might become nasty. Blue and golds deserve the highest praise. They are said to be somewhat more intelligent

For many, the blue and gold is the quintessential macaw: they are good pets, beautiful birds, and even good breeders.

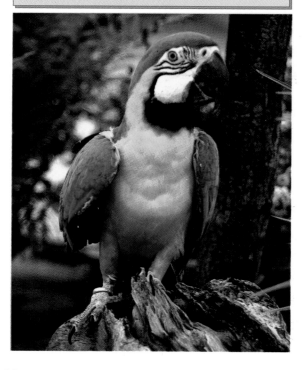

and alert than other species. Definitely curious, these birds have a knack for getting into mischief. They are among the better talkers. Many bird handlers consider the blue and gold to be the gentlest and most trainable of the macaws. This species tends to become attached to one person or sex, usually shying away from strangers. Naturally affectionate, the blue and gold makes a devoted pet.

Blue and gold macaws, like all other macaws, should be housed in a strong aviary where the wood is protected from their gnawing. In the winter it is essential to house them indoors, but no artificial heat is needed.

Crossings of the blue and gold macaw include:

Blue and gold X green-winged.

Blue and gold X scarlet.

Scarlet Macaw

The scarlet macaw, *Ara macao* (Linnaeus), also referred to as the red and yellow, is probably one of the most breathtaking parrots you will ever see. It is a large bird growing to a length of approximately 36 inches, nearly half of which is a long tapering tail. The hen is similar but slightly smaller, with a shorter, broader beak. The overall coloring of the scarlet is deep radiant red. The wings are bright yellow and blue. The rump is light blue. Its tail is a

As a blue and gold macaw grows older, its black facial feathers become more sharply defined.

deep shade of blue mixed with red. The scarlet's cheek patch is flesh-colored, and the beak is whitish on the upper mandible and black on the lower mandible.

These beautiful creatures are found in southern Mexico, Central America, and northwestern sections of South America. They are most comfortable in light woodland rather than humid forests.

Scarlet macaws are very sociable birds and are usually seen in pairs, family parties, or flocks of up to 30. There is a deep bond between pairs. They can be spotted in flocks, flying side by side, their wings nearly touching. The birds leave their roost during the day in search of food, which is found in treetops. Their diet consists of seeds, fruits, nuts, and berries. When night falls they return home. Little is known of their breeding habits other than they nest in the hollows of trees.

In captivity the scarlet is one of the more popular macaws, not only because of its beautiful plumage, but also for the dedication it bestows on the one who cares for it. This bird has the ability to speak clearly and, surprisingly enough, it is less expensive than some of the other popular species.

The scarlet has perhaps one real drawback, an earth-

Because they can be tamed to be easily handled, scarlet macaws are the favorite of many.

shattering screech. As one disgruntled owner so poetically put it, "A scarlet can shatter glass from a mile away." There is one saving grace: Macaws usually only scream at certain times of the day or when they are bored or frustrated. If you are prepared to give your bird the proper attention it deserves, you will undoubtedly be rewarded with a loving, affectionate pet.

Scarlet macaws love to bathe and have been observed to sit in a light rain, slapping themselves and maneuvering their bodies so as to wet themselves all over, much like humans behave in the shower.

An extremely large nest box should be provided all year long because the scarlet macaw will like to roost in the nest box as well as use it for breeding purposes. It would be wise to protect the corners from gnawing of the birds by reinforcing them with metal strips.

There are a few known crossings of the scarlet macaw, which include:
Scarlet X military.
Scarlet X blue and gold.
Scarlet X green winged.

Green Winged Macaw

The green winged macaw, *Ara chloroptera* (G.R. Gray), has a number of other names that often lead to confusion: red and blue macaw, red and green macaw, crimson macaw, and the maroon macaw. Try to keep in mind if you come across these names that they are all referring to the same bird.

The plumage of the green winged is very similar to the scarlet, with these exceptions: it is a deeper shade of red and the wings are dark green and blue instead of yellow and blue. The cheek patch is whitish with a trace of red feathers lining the face. The tail, which is shorter than the scarlet's, is blue splashed with deep red. The beak is horn white on the upper mandible, with the lower mandible black. The green winged has a large head and beak and a very stocky body. It grows to be approximately 32 inches long.

This macaw is most often found in the hilly country of eastern Panama and in many areas of South America. Like the scarlet, the green winged

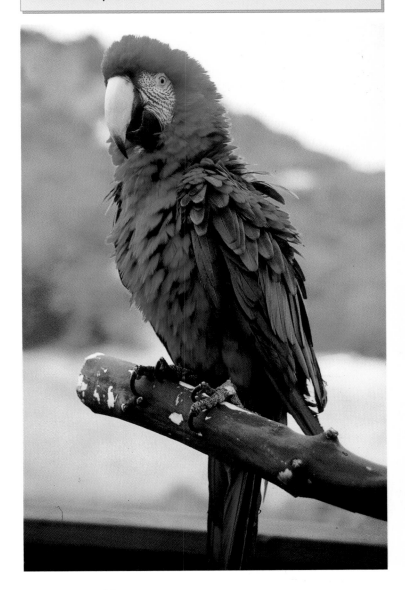

The green winged macaw, with its brilliant red, green, and blue coloring, makes a wonderful companion.

Though it is sometimes confused with the scarlet macaw, the green winged is a larger bird with rows of tiny red feathers on its facial patch.

is seldom seen along the coast. It prefers the forests of the interior.

This species is very much like the other large macaws except that they usually travel in pairs or small parties, not in flocks. During the nesting season, green wings live in pairs. The hen usually lays two eggs, sometimes three. The young hatch in 24 to 26 days. They leave the nest at three months, at which time they resemble the parents except that they have shorter tails.

This species is no longer readily available and is therefore very expensive. However, their temperature is much like that of the hyacinth. They get along very well with children and pets. The green winged macaw has been bred successfully in captivity and has proved to make excellent parents. The green winged macaw is easily frightened by sudden movements and noises, therefore it is advisable to

keep them in a fairly quiet environment. Remember that it is the instinctive reaction of a frightened macaw to bite.

This macaw was first bred in England in 1962, by J.S. Riff. From 1962 to 1968, they bred almost annually so that by 1968 he had reared 13 young.

Buffon's macaw (*Ara ambigua*) is often mistaken for the military macaw; however, the Buffon is generally larger, with a more greenish-yellow neck than a military.

Military Macaw

The military macaw or great green macaw, *Ara militaris militaris* (Linnaeus), grows to a length of approximately 27 inches; the hen is slightly smaller. This bird is an overall olive green color. It has a deep red forehead, black beak, bluish red primary feathers, and a tail that is olive yellow on the under surface and brownish red on the upper surface. The cheek patch is whitish with rows of violet brown feathers.

The military is easily tamed and has a moderate talking ability. However, due to its comparatively dull coloring it has never gained the same

popularity as the macaws previously mentioned. Some authorities feel that the military's personality is not quite up to par with the other species. For these reasons the military macaw is relatively inexpensive.

The military macaw is found in Mexico, the northwestern part of tropical South America, and the tropical parts of Bolivia to the Argentine border. These birds are happiest in dry forest and open woodland, and they try to avoid tropical rainforest. They usually travel in pairs or in flocks of up to 20. This is quite different from some other macaws that only live in pairs. Their habits are similar to the scarlet macaw's. They leave their roost in the early morning in search of food and return home at night. Their diet consists of seeds, nuts, berries, fruits, and vegetable matter. When resting, they perch on the tops of very tall trees.

The coloring of the blue-throated macaw (*Ara glaucogularis*) is similar to that of the more common blue and gold.

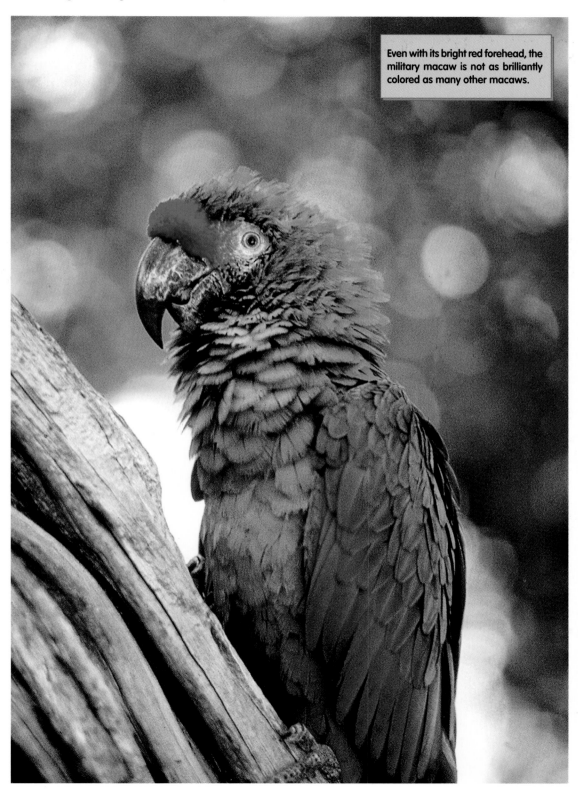

Even with its bright red forehead, the military macaw is not as brilliantly colored as many other macaws.

DWARF MACAWS

Severe Macaw

The severe macaw, *Ara severa severa* (Linnaeus), is one of the most popular of the dwarf macaws. It is also one of the most frequently available. The plumage of the severe greatly resembles that of the military macaw; however, this energetic little creature only grows to a length of approximately 20 inches.

The severe macaw is almost entirely dark green. Its crown is blue and its forehead deep brown at the base of the upper mandible. Its bare white cheek patch has a small trace of feathers. The flight feathers and upper side of the tail are blue mixed with green. Underwing coverts are red. The under side of the severe's tail is red mixed with brown; beak and feet are black. The proportions of this species are much more appealing than that of the military macaw.

The severe macaw's natural habitat ranges from eastern Panama to the Guianas, south to northern Bolivia and in southern Brazil. They are frequently seen in tropical forest zones. The natural call of these parrots is higher pitched than the larger macaws. Their cries also seem to have a complaining ring.

The severe nests high up in the hollows of dead trees. The hen usually lays a single egg. In captivity severes make loving and affectionate pets. They possess all of the charm of their cousins, but are somewhat easier to accommodate due to their smaller size. They can live contentedly in a large cage, but should be allowed out for extra exercise.

It is difficult to select a pair of severes for mating purposes, just as it is with most other species, due to the similarity of plumage between the sexes. However, if

Many owners prefer the severe macaws because their smaller size makes them easier to care for.

you do buy a mated pair, they can be kept in a small sturdy aviary and should be able to breed. A nesting box for this species should be 16 inches high, 16 inches wide, and have a 16-inch circular entrance. Damp soil and a little moss should be placed on the bottom of the box to allow for sufficient moisture to keep the eggs from becoming too dry. You can expect to find two or three eggs that should hatch in approximately 28 days. The young will remain in the nest for about seven weeks after fledging and will still be fed by the parents.

Since the severe is a dwarf macaw it has some special food requirements. They should be fed canary seed, millet, hemp, and some greens and branches.

The severe macaw is quite sensitive to cold and drafts, therefore it is advisable to

Nuts should not be your severe macaw's primary source of nutrition; greens, hemp, millet, and canary seeds are also important.

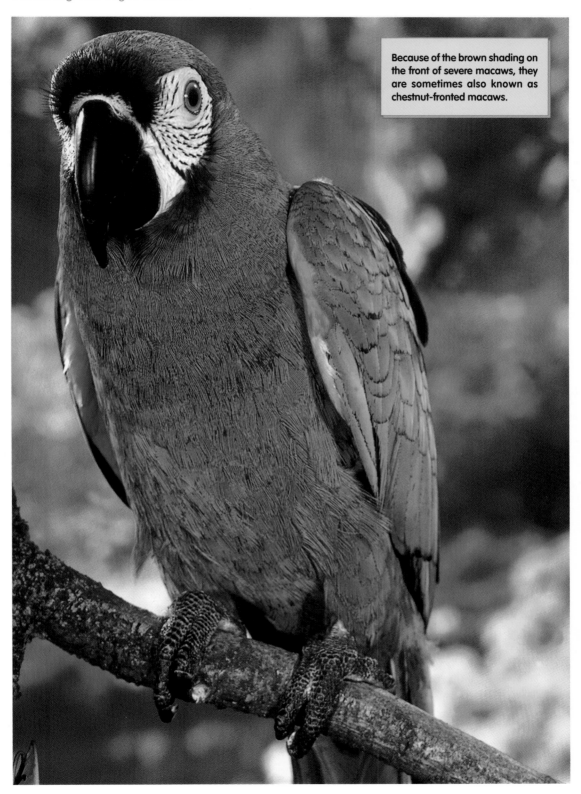

Because of the brown shading on the front of severe macaws, they are sometimes also known as chestnut-fronted macaws.

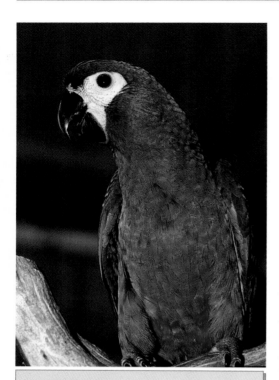

With its red forehead, bluish-green cheeks and throat, and bright red abdomen, the Illiger's macaw is one of the more colorful dwarf macaws.

Illiger's macaw is a native of eastern Brazil and northeastern Argentina. It is a bird of the forest, found particularly in areas near waterways. It is usually seen in pairs or small parties. Unlike other miniature macaws, this bird has a distinctive flight pattern. It does not fly straight and true, but rather jerks up in flight in a bucking motion. Its natural call is a deep guttural screech.

snap. Otherwise, they make fine pets.

The Illiger's macaw needs a nest box of approximately 15 inches by 15 inches in order to have any chance of breeding. They will also use this nest box year-round to roost in. In the opinion of Dr. M. Vriends, breeding successes are gently improved if they are fed all year on bits of bread soaked in milk. The young in the nest should be fed on a high protein diet.

Yellow-Naped Macaw

The yellow-naped macaw, *Ara auricollis* (Cassin), also referred to as the yellow-collared, is another member of the green dwarf macaws. This species grows to a length of about 16 to 18 inches. It is basically dark green with a

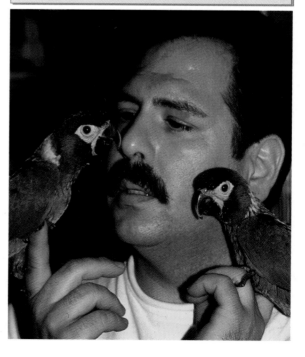

As a pet, the yellow-naped macaw (also known as yellow-collared) is very adaptable and makes a pleasant companion.

winter them inside with some artificial heat.

Illiger's Macaw

The Illiger's macaw, *Ara maracana* (Vieillot), is somewhat similar to the severe, but it only grows to a length of 17 inches. The overall coloring is an olive green. Its forehead is orange red, followed by a bluish green head. The Illiger's has a red patch on its belly and lower back. Wings are blue and green; the tail is blue. Its eyes are a reddish brown, the cheek patch and cere are yellow. Its beak is blackish brown and its legs are flesh-colored. The hen is basically the same in coloring except that the red on its forehead is duller.

This species adjusts very well to captivity. They quickly become tame and are extremely affectionate. Unlike some other birds, they love to be petted. However, they have a tendency to be moody and they occasionally lose their temper and

Red-bellied macaws can be identified by a naked yellow cheek patch and a large red area on the abdomen.

black forehead and an attractive yellow collar on the back of its neck. The primary and secondary feathers, along with the tail feathers, are splashed with blue. The cheek patch is white. The eyes are reddish and its beak is black.

The yellow-naped macaw is a native of eastern Bolivia, Paraguay, several areas of Argentina, and some parts of Brazil. They are plentiful in swamplands and are seen most frequently in flocks. In captivity the yellow-naped has a sharp, high-pitched screech.

They make excellent pets and are known for their endearing and clownish behavior, especially in the morning. This species, along with the other dwarf macaws, is considerably less expensive than the larger macaws. This makes them attractive to the

bird fancier who can't afford to purchase a large macaw, but is intrigued by the personalities of these magnificent parrots.

Red Bellied Macaw

The name of this miniature macaw, *Ara manilata* (Boddaert), red bellied, is very misleading because the bird only has a faint trace of red on its belly. If anything, this bird should rightly be called the black headed macaw. Basically green, the red-bellied macaw's forehead is black, followed by bluish green on the nape of its neck. Primary flight feathers are blue with black tips. The tail has a dull reddish tinge on the upper side and a light yellow tinge on the under side. Its beak is dark but lighter at the tips.

Even without the bright coloring of such macaws as the striking scarlets and hyacinths, the red-bellied macaws still make good pets.

Although noble macaws can be noisy at times, they are quite friendly once trained.

It is a native of southeastern Venezuela and northeastern Peru and Brazil. They are typically found in palm swamps and usually live in pairs or small groups. These macaws like to rest during the day and then become active in the afternoon around four o'clock. They are not very sociable, but they occasionally associate with orange-winged amazons. Little else is known of their habits in the wild. They are quite rare and seen very infrequently in captivity. This species was imported into Europe in 1872 (Amsterdam Zoo "Artis"). There is no record of the species having bred in captivity.

Noble Macaw

This adorable little creature, *Ara nobilis cumanensis* (Lichtenstein), is the smallest of all macaws, growing to a length of only 12 inches. It is sometimes confused with the blue crowned conure. Its one identifying mark is its bare cheek patch.

The noble macaw is an overall dull green. Its underwings are red, the flight feathers splashed with black. Its beak is also black. The crown and forehead of the noble macaw are bluish, and its five-inch tail is tinged with yellow.

These petite macaws are found in the Guianas, eastern Venezuela, and southern Brazil. They are generally encountered in flocks that are easily detected because they are very noisy birds and screech loudly while in flight. In captivity, these birds easily become tame and are very gentle. They make lovely pets and are famous for their mimicry.

The birds are available on the American and European market from time to time, but the first record of breeding in captivity dates from 1949 (Vane, England). The noble macaw was first exhibited in Berlin in 1879.

Noble macaws, also called red-shouldered, are the smallest of the dwarf macaws.

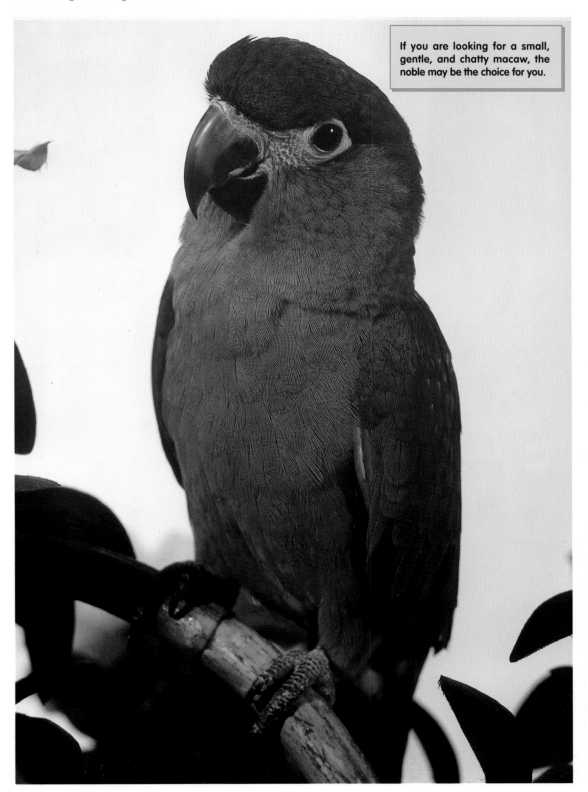

If you are looking for a small, gentle, and chatty macaw, the noble may be the choice for you.

Suggested Reading

H-1079
The World of Macaws

By Dieter Hoppe
The World of Macaws details the natural history and distribution of 26 different macaws; the book's 144 pages are handsomely illustrated with 96 full-color drawing and photographs.

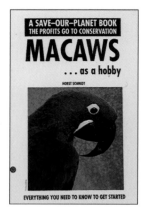

TT-039
Macaws as a Hobby

By Horst Schmidt
With more than 60 full-color photographs, this 98-page book describes the varying species of macaws and provides valuable information about breeding.

H-1044
Handbook of Macaws

By Dr. A.E. Decoteau
Macaw owners, naturalists, and bird fanciers will find this informative book a useful reference tool, especially for its species classifications and training advice; 128 pages.

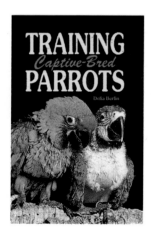

TS-242
Training Captive-Bred Parrots

By Delia Berlin
The joy of keeping captive-bred parrots is brought to life in this 128-page book; includes chapters on buying a baby, preventing health problems, and training.

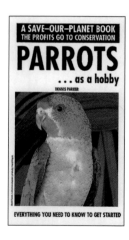

TT-037
Parrots as a Hobby

By Dennis Parker
This 98-page book covers everything a new parrot owner needs to know to get started: selecting the right bird, accommodations, feeding, breeding, and health care.